# YOUR LOVED ONE IS TALKING,
# PLEASE LISTEN!

*Written by the Vick Men —*

JOACHIEM, MICAIAH, ZECHARIAH
AND SHIRON VICK

Copyright © 2017 by Joachiem, Micaiah, Zechariah and Shiron Vick

*Your loved one is talking, please listen!*
by Joachiem, Micaiah, Zechariah and Shiron Vick

Printed in the United States of America.

ISBN 9781498496506

All rights reserved solely by the author. The author guarantees all contents are original and do not infringe upon the legal rights of any other person or work. No part of this book may be reproduced in any form without the permission of the author. The views expressed in this book are not necessarily those of the publisher.

Unless otherwise indicated, Scripture quotations taken from the King James Version (KJV) – *public domain.*

www.xulonpress.com

# Contents

Introduction.........................................vii
Acknowledgement......................................ix

| | | |
|---|---|---|
| Letter1. | A letter to the Church ................ 11 | |
| | To Whom Much is Given | |
| | Let This Mind Be In You | |
| | Fan Or Follower | |
| | Relationships- Am I My Brother's Keeper? | |
| | The Tree | |
| | In-a-me (enemy) in the gate | |
| | Samson Syndrome | |
| | Anger | |
| Letter2. | A letter to the Pastor ................ 25 | |
| Letter3. | A letter to the Man.................... 28 | |
| | Fear | |
| | Like-Mindedness | |
| | Identity Crisis | |
| Letter4. | A letter to the Woman ................ 31 | |
| Letter5. | A letter to the Parent ................ 33 | |

# Introduction

Grace and peace be unto you from God the Father and the Lord Jesus Christ. This collection of letters is written to the people who seek to serve the Lord. In serving our God, there are many times that we fall short and wish others understood the trials of our individual lives and were there to hear our thoughts. To the men and women of God who are our shepherds, who may read this work and take offense, I ask that you forgive us. We are saying what most people would like to speak. This book is also penned to those on the sideline who question why we serve God and those who want salvation through Jesus Christ but are hindered by life, and to my sons and the young men and women warriors of our Lord and Savior Jesus Christ.

# Acknowledgement

Thank you Archbishop Roy E. Brown and Archbishop Robert Rochford. Thank you, Pastor Deborah Crowe, Pastor Andy Thompson and Pastor Kenneth and First Lady Beverly Porter. Very special thanks to Archbishop George M. Shorts. I appreciate you. You were my pastor, but you will always be my family.

The Word says "and there is a friend that sticketh closer than a brother."[1] Tarik (Todd) Simon, Gary Joseph, Dave Pearson, Tracy Green and Derek Singleton, you are those friends. Anthony and Fu, thanks for being my family and a friend. Thanks for sharpening my iron.

Gina, thank you for being my biggest encourager and for reminding me to write. I have many cousins, but Shirika, Charnette and Robin, you are my friends. I have aunts on both sides of my family who I love, like Robbin and Mona; however, Aunt Shirley, you have and will always hold a very special place in my life.

Thanks, Big E. Eric, you always call me your older brother, but you have always been the best friend and older brother a man could want. I have always been able to count on you to be honest with me, to speak the words of life through the Word of God and to listen to me. Throughout the tough times in our lives, I have always been able to say I trust you. The past forty-five years of our friendship have been a blessing. Thanks for sharpening my iron.

---

[1] Proverbs 18:24b

Jay, I need you. I am waiting for you.

Meme (La-Kisha) you are a godsend. You are a great sister, and I love and honor you so much. I appreciate you as a prayer and business partner and as a friend. I appreciate the dedication you have to helping others and the love you have shown us. I see your strength as a black woman, but also as one who submits to the precepts of the Word. You have grown to be a great woman of our God. Thanks for sharpening my iron.

Nana, I touch and agree with you for one hundred years of life. I have watched you feed the men and women of God and our family who comes into town. You have supplied us with food and your love. When our mother and father departed this realm, you stepped in and became our support and backbone in so many ways. Nana, I love and cherish you greatly. Thanks for being a good Christian.

Thank you, Mom, for always being a woman of God who trained me how to seek and serve Christ. Thank you also for teaching me to communicate through any emotion and to never be ashamed of who I was. Throughout my life with you, you always encouraged me to express my feelings; I remember many of our conversations, often in the night, where I knew I was loved and accepted. Mom, you modeled the life of a true believer, and your crown awaits you. Thanks for telling me I had iron and for sharpening it. Lord, I bless and praise your holy name and thank you for the gift of Evelyn Vick. I appreciate your blessings through Mom. Father, I love you.

I am truly blessed and honored to have my seeds join me in completing this book. Without your wisdom and guidance, these words would not appear on paper. Praise belongs to the Most High for your life. You helped me remain focused in spite of the trials of our lives, and many words cannot express how great a love we possess. It has always been my pleasure to serve you as your father. Thanks for looking up to me and believing in me. Your prayers helped us prevail and conquer. I am proud to be your dad. God bless you, and I love you. So, Zech, Kia, and Joa, my mighty men of valor, here we go.

# A letter to the Church

Father God, in the name of Jesus I ask that you forgive your people for walking in fear, for walking in pride and for being disobedient when we hear your voice. We seek your forgiveness.

Am I my brother's keeper? Do we have everything in common? Have we fallen away from the principles that caused the early church in the New Testament to grow? Are we as one body, one local church, one individual believer, doing our part to carry out the Great Commission?

I have to repent for not doing my part. One can easily get caught up in being a religionist. On Sundays we attend church, and we go to weekly Bible study or service when it is convenient to our schedule. We live moral lifestyles, but have no power. When those outside of the church see us, what do they see? Do they see an individual presenting love and compassion? Do they see Christ in us? As I write this, I also have had to repent for my actions for hindering the message of salvation. Those of us who have been raised in the church or have been in the way for a long time often become complacent because we understand the culture. We know what words to say and when to say them. We understand what our posture should be and what rules we should seemingly follow. To the average stranger, we seem to be good people, but . . .

Do we know one another? Do we have everything in common? Do we share our lives with the other believers in our sanctuary, or do we remain distant from others and face the attack of the enemy alone?

Men are guiltier of this conduct than women. Brothers, we will sit in our homes and go half crazy instead of opening up to another person. Most of the time, we all go through some of the same trials that could have been avoided if we expressed ourselves to someone else. Often they have experienced a similar test and by sharing our testimony with the success and shortcomings, sin or hardships, a lot of heartache can be avoided. When we trust another believer, we gain a partner and a fellow warrior. I learned that life lesson a few years.

During one of the worse times in my life, I broke my standard pattern of isolation and accepted the strength of other men. I was transformed. These men loved me and nursed me back to spiritual and mental health. I am grateful that the Lord touched those five men to minister grace and life to me. They refuse to allow me to indulge in pity or to give up. I recall my cousin Anthony once saying, "You can't die, we need you." Whether it was Dave reminding me that I was a good man, or Gary giving me wisdom, or Todd checking my walk, or Fu feeding me, my brothers in Christ sustained me in all manners. **Iron can only sharpen iron if we show our swords.**

## **TO WHOM MUCH IS GIVEN.**

"To whom much is given, much is required."[2] Too often we, men, women, believers, hear this saying and think that we have not been given much. Perhaps you may have experienced a lot of tragedy in your life and lost, but you have been given a lot. Perhaps death visited your family more often than the next. Maybe you have been divorced or are a child of the divorced parent, and your world has been turned upside down. Perhaps finances are always small, and you do not like your way of life. You may have experienced church hurt, and now you wander around looking for a place of peace in which to seek our Lord. To whom much is given, much is required.

There are those of us in life that have been blessed with abounding faith in which, despite all negatives of life, still press forward; we still love our families, we go to work and church with smiles, and we still

---

[2] " Luke 12:48b

trust God no matter what has happened. You, I, and others w_
have had rough lives have been given much. We have the s_____
endure. Some who faced the same trials as you may be dead, mentally
imprisoned, in a mental institution, on the streets or in a boardroom
selling their lives for financial gain. You are blessed because Christ
has given you much.

Much is the faith to believe one day your situation will change. Much means succeeding in spite of coming from a single-parent home. Much means coming from one of the most violent neighborhoods in your city, but you still graduate, and you are alive. Much means believing in yourself. Much means enduring the pain, tears and doubts, but experiencing your victory. You are a winner. You are more than a conqueror. You are a great leader. It has never been about what you may have been told or seen, but what you know deep down inside of your heart: "ARISE, shine; for thy light is come, and the glory of the LORD is risen upon thee. For, behold, the darkness shall cover the earth, and gross darkness the people: but the LORD shall arise upon thee, and his glory shall be seen upon thee."[3] "Your path has already been determined, and nothing shall deny you access. Much has been given to you but you must believe that "greater is he that is in you, then he that is in the world."[4]

However, because much has been given to you, you are also required to fulfill the Great Commission.

## **LET THIS MIND BE IN YOU.**

Society and negative influence have guided a lot of what we think about ourselves and our pictures of success. I, like most people, once bought into the so-called image of success. I had to have the new fly SUV with the big home in the suburbs. My wife and sons had to dress in the name-brand clothing of the moment. I needed to be around select people because that meant I was "it" or on the way to being "it." I ate at certain restaurants not because the food was always better,

---

[3] Isaiah 60:1,2

[4] I John 4:4

but because the dictates of society positioned me with a thought pattern to think that a particular class of individuals does certain things. Does this sound familiar? There is absolutely nothing wrong with wanting and having "nice" things, but is your mind programmed to think that you are not successful, or you can only achieve success if you have or can obtain individual possessions?

According to society, I was considered to be successful. I had a huge home, nice car, pretty wife and money in the bank. I was a leader in my church, my sons were great athletes, and my business was making money. People looked up to me, wanted to be around me—but I was not fulfilling my mandate. Too often we base our lives on the materials we possess instead of what kind of character we have. Sometimes we get lost in this noisy world and forget who we are. It was after I lost just about everything that I remembered I still have much more. The Bible says, "let this mind be in you, which was also in Christ Jesus."[5]

Who are you? What do you believe about yourself? You are alive because you refuse to surrender to a defeated mind. True, life has not been pretty. You have experienced more down days than bright sun. Your money laughs at you. Life has been a roller coaster for a long time, but you can take it—not only because you have to, but because you are built for it. Have you yet to realize that you are a warrior? No one can endure the things you have, and yet here you are. "Let this mind be in you," which was also in Christ Jesus.[6] Christ walked this earth knowing who he was, his purpose, and how the story would end. Do you know how successfully your life story will be written? Do you conduct life affairs with a prosperous mindset? "For as he thinketh in his heart, so is he." [7] What we believe about ourselves will portray what will become. Jesus walked the earth with a purpose. They said, *is not he the carpenter's son*? They also said, *no good thing comes out of Galilee*. Where was Jesus born? He and his parents were homeless. Does this sound familiar to you? What is being

---

[5] " Philippians 2:5

[6] " Philippians 2:5

[7] Proverbs 23:7a

said about you? Where were you born? Perhaps you have heard you are black or fat or have a criminal record. They may have said that you are white trash or short or ugly or not good enough. Someone somewhere has attempted to place a label on you. They did it to Christ, but what did he do with that label? He went on to become the greatest man that ever will live. *Who* are you?

The Bible states, "Therefore if any man be in Christ, he is a new creature: old things are passed away; behold all things are become new."[8] When we were first saved, it was such a beautiful thing. We wanted to tell the whole world about the God we met and how He has come into our life. If we sinned, we were quick to confess our shortcomings, and it meant everything to walk right before the Lord. If someone told us that we offended them, we were willing to make things right with the person so the trespass would be abated. Now, I find that some believers choose not to walk in the principles of Christ and ask for forgiveness when they harm others with our words or actions. The Bible says, "if we confess our sins, he is faithful and just to forgive us our sins, and to cleanse us from all unrighteousness."[9] These are some of the things I have heard people say: I'm not asking God to forgive me, because I'm just going to do it again. I'm not asking anyone to forgive me because they will not. I am mad with that person, so I do not forgive them. They do the same thing time after time after time.

I remember when I was growing up, my mother taught us not to live with excuses. She said that making excuses will only hinder you from acknowledging the truth and prevent your progress. Mom said, "Ron, walk in truth and righteousness." I hope that we have not become an excuse-generated church.

## **FAN OR FOLLOWER.**[10]
Am I a Christian, or a person who just believes in Jesus Christ? Am I sanctified, or am I a hypocrite? If a stranger entered your home

---

[8] II Corinthians 5:17

[9] 1 John 1:9

[10] Sermon preached by Pastor Kenneth Porter

and asked your spouse or child if you were a Christian, what would they say? If someone asked the same question to your co-workers or extended family, what would be the response of those people? The Word describes a Christian as someone who acts like Christ. So are you a Christian or someone who just attends a church occasionally?

In our churches, homes, jobs and every area of life, the bible states we are supposed to be the light.[11] But what do people say about you? Why is it in the church (the body of Christ) we have so many divorces and the children of believers leaving the church? The answer can come in many forms. First, the person never honestly confesses the sin in his or her life. Alternatively they could be spiritually fighting demons that have been in the bloodline. Or perhaps the person would rather walk around believers and suffer defeat upon defeat instead of walk victoriously as the Lord desires for our lives.

When I moved to North Carolina, I attended a great church for a season. It was there that I met my wife and some great men and women of God. I am not one who is surprised or shocked often, however the believers there have my prayers. I was called a Bible thumper because I spoke the Word. People would say that they did not want to be in a traditional church, and a person would put down another person by saying you are holier than thou or a holy roller. Now I know some of you are shaking your head because I thought we were supposed to be holy (different).[12] My experiences there also led me to the church I worship at now.

It is my understanding, like most of you, that the believer must strive to act differently from the rest of the world, right? That does not mean that you cannot be cool or real or down to earth. It also does not mean you cannot have fun and go out and enjoy life. Our conduct should be governed by the Word of God, and the Word sets the standard for what is right and wrong. So ask yourself, *am I a fan or a follower?*

---

[11] Matthew 5:14

[12] 1 Peter 2:9

My understanding from Pastor Ken's sermon is simple: either we are following what Christ said and following the precepts of the Bible, or we are conducting our lives as fans. A fan is someone who goes to church occasionally, or even every Sunday, but who does not submit his or her life to the Lordship of Jesus Christ. A fan is someone whose light of salvation has gone dim. A fan is someone who is more concerned about trends of the world than the movement of the Holy Spirit. A church made up of fans quashes the unction of the Holy Spirit. I decide not to be a part-time follower.

## **RELATIONSHIPS- AM I MY BROTHER'S KEEPER?**

I am stronger now because of the love Christ put in men for me. When I was battling with my salvation over twenty years ago, Derek banged on my bedroom door and stalked me until I came back to church. When I decided to rededicate my life to Christ in my early twenties, it was a real battle. I was fighting a sex spirit and wanted to be with my girlfriend sexually every day. I was also fighting my lust for money. I was not earning much at work, and a lot of my friends in the street were making $1000 to $3000 weekly. I was also fighting anger and the spirit of death. Two years before my decision to fully follow Christ, my youngest brother was murdered. He was not only my blood brother, but also my best friend. Although I was a "working man", I walked around plotting revenge and how I could kill everybody related to his death. At the time I was not married, and I did not have any children, so I did not care whether I lived or died.

I was in the midst of an intense spiritual and mental battle. I shared a home with my sister and cousin, and they did not know how to reach me. I had such a crazed look in my eyes. I was *really* in the midst of an intense spiritual and mental battle. I was fighting for my life and my salvation. When I was not walking the streets looking for death or sex or money, I was in my room conducting spiritual warfare. I would fast a few times a week and pray for hours each night. I am telling my personal testimony because often in our churches, we fail to discern spiritually and see that others need a lifeline. They may not be facing what I endured because each one of us has different grace, but loneliness is loneliness and stress is stress. I thank God for the brothers who did not know me at the time bearing my burdens and praying me through.

When my family fell apart through a divorce, Todd, Gary, and Dave took turns reminding me that I was a man of God and became my strength. Throughout my life, Eric has given me honest, Godly advice and walked with me. Where are the rest of my brothers? I know a lot of you are out there, but our women can't see you. Now it was not for me to use them as a crutch, but I am grateful that when the toughest times of my life came, I had powerful men of valor to hold me down. However, bearing another's burden is not just reserved for the individual believer.

Too often many churches, especially in the inner cities, share a street or neighborhood with one or more other churches. Every Sunday and Wednesday (Bible study or prayer night) we see others pass by us with their families, and we enter into separate buildings. Sometimes we are neighborly and wave hello, but for the most part, we rarely if ever interact. Our pastors know the name of the other pastor, but that is it. Because we are in the same zip code we share the same spiritual attacks, social issues and sometimes the same families, but why do we rarely join forces and sharpen one another's iron? Now I know you thought about your denomination, right? But we serve the same risen savior.

My church was guilty of closed fellowship. In Brooklyn, you pass one hundred churches before you get to your street. It is a shame, yet this is the practice of many churches across America. Now some of us do fellowship with our friends in the gospel. Your congregation visits their congregation, and the same preachers visit. Cool, there is nothing wrong with sharing with those you know and love, but isn't our love called to be greater shared than just with the known?

I once heard a pastor say that we are working in the same vineyard. That is a true saying and many churches understand the concept and often partner with other churches they know little about and spread the gospel. In reading the book of Acts, the gospel was spread by the believers having "everything in common."[13] I applaud the many brothers and sisters in this practice of love, but the Lord forgives those of us who are falling short.

## **THE TREE**.

Have you ever heard the saying "the apple did not fall far from the tree"? Because of blessings and curses that may be in the family line, the believer has to contend with spiritual wickedness assigned to that family. For instance, if the grandfather or father was alcoholic, the son may be an alcoholic unless that cord is destroyed spiritually. If the grandmother or mother does not have respect for men, the daughter will not show her husband respect unless she is delivered from that characteristic. My pastor once said that we have to be careful not to allow the enemy into our homes and I agree, but I take this assessment further. The enemy works comfortably in our home unless we confront those spirits and cast them out.

I feel that for the Christian to walk victoriously, we have to acknowledge honestly the demons or imps assigned to our families. The epistle to the Romans reminds us that we wrestle not against flesh and blood, but against spiritual wickedness in high places.[14] We are at war and Ephesians 6:10-18 advises us how to adorn ourselves for battle.

However, who do you resemble? Christ stated, "if you see me, you see the father."[15] Do we strive to act like our heavenly father or earthly people? Are we as a church, the called out, redeemed people, willing to shed the identity and labels we accepted from society? You know what I am saying: A pastor is supposed to look and act a certain way. A man has to be strong and not show any emotions (when a woman is strong as and just as good as a man). We have placed in boxes what Black, White, Hispanic and Asian Christians are sup-

---

[13] Acts 2:44:Acts 4:32

[14] Ephesians 6:12

[15] " John 14:9

posed to be. The list can go on and on. Is there not One Church? I always asked myself *why are there so many different denominations?* We all believe that Jesus Christ is God in the flesh, and He rose from the dead, right? When Christ returns, He is coming back for one church, right? So what's up with all the division? I should act like my brother in the other church, and we both should act like Christ.

## **IN-A-ME (ENEMY) IN THE GATE.**

All too often in our homes and in our churches, the enemy (In-a-me) resides inside the gates. We know of the enemy's presence, and we are very comfortable with the destruction because the enemy is us. As believers, we have become so entrenched in the standards of the world that we use the doctrine of grace as a scapegoat. When has the grace of our Lord given us a get out of jail free card to sin? What has happened to us where some have now become so proud and selfish that no one can advise us of our faults, or has love evaporated to the point where some turn a blind eye to the sin of their neighbor because they are afraid to bear another person's burden? Hopefully we are not becoming a lawless society of believers because some feel that the precepts of God are no longer relevant in this age of time.

In the last decade, I have witnessed so many homes being damaged by divorce. Mine is one of them. Husbands do not love their wives like Christ, and the women refuse to submit to the husbands. We go to church, and some of us read God's Word, yet all too often most of us refuse to follow the precepts. However, what is most disturbing in this sin for all, is some pastors encourage the conduct because they do not want to lose members or friendships. Have we become a feelings-based church or do we have what it takes to conquer through the spirit? I know that the Spirit of the Lord will always prevail, yet how much more division must be we suffer until we, as a collective body, defeat the true enemy: ourselves. The truth in the Word of God can make us free if we so desire.

Men, man up and stop leaving the place of leadership to a woman. Do you know who you are? Do you understand that your life in God is not conditioned by how much money you have or what position you hold? Please get out of your feelings and off the chair of do nothing. Take up your mantle and stop waiting for the destroyer to steal and kill. Now some of us are about our Father's business, and we too fall short, so if you are not afraid to lead or speak up, then I am not talking to you. If you are a male who does not exercise his authority and allows everything (his woman, lack of money, confidence, fear of being alone and guilt) to usurp your authority, we need to talk and together let's get in our place. Our women and children need and expect us to lead.

And women, cut it out. If you are married, stop being the vessel of the destroyer against your man. The plot of the *real* enemy is to use you to bring down that man so the family and territory of God has for the two of you can be destroyed. Some of you seem to be more controlled by your feelings than the spirit of Christ. Your attitude or misconception that you are as strong as a man is not going to secure his love or whip him into shape. He needs and desires your respect and commitment. Please, please leave that feminist movement out of the church and your life. You can still be spiritually strong but gentle. You can still have success in life without being a cutthroat or one of the boys.

## **SAMSON SYNDROME.**

I submit that often many believers fall into what I consider as the Samson syndrome. We all know the story in the book of **Judges Chapter 16** about the great judge, Samson, who shook himself for strength unaware that the spirit of the Lord had departed from him. Samson was so used to going about life expecting that the Lord would always be with him. I confess that I was once guilty of this syndrome.

There was a time years ago when I did not hear the voice of the Lord, nor did I feel his presence—and it scared me. I was shook. I did not know exactly when he departed from me. I read my Word, I prayed, I was faithful in ministry and I lived pretty much a sinless life. I was used to the presence of the Lord being with me. I knew when to turn left or right. I think I may have taken the Lord's presence for granted and quenched the spirit. When one is working in ministry or walking in "your gift", you have to be very careful. As believers sometimes we get caught up in "ministry" or "serving" and neglect to stay tuned into the Holy Spirit. We operate out of our gifts and because we are "being used" assume that we are pleasing to God. It's not until we get into real trouble and need the Lord's guidance and power that we realize the anointing has left us.

I am blessed that the spirit returned to me, but how many of us go to church and are involved in ministry still unsure of what the Lord wants from us? It's easy to get caught up in the cares or life and forget that our Master must remain the focus of all we do. The plot of the enemy is not to drive believers away from church, but to cause a person to become backslidden while attending church or even functioning in ministry. No matter what takes place in their lives, most saints will never stop going to church. They know that some way they must continue to press on either because they love the Lord, or they love the tradition (every week they are in their place). Without an anointing, without the power of the Spirit, you are still missing the mark. Without the spirit of the Lord dwelling in us and guiding us daily, who knows what we are capable of doing. If we are not prayerful, a religionist or noble spirit can overtake you. You know what I am saying: morality.

Today it seems that a lot of believers are walking in morality. To clarify, you should obey the laws of the land, do no harm to anyone and do your best to be truthful. However, the moral spirit is deceiving because a person can be a good citizen who follows what most consider being right, but still not adhere to the gospel. For example, as believers one can live a lawful life yet, feel biblical mandates are too archaic and should not be followed. As believers, we have to submit to natural laws. However, the mandate of Christ for our individual and corporate lives should never be taken lightly. I pray that the Lord forgives us because it is very easy to lose sight. Let us be mindful that Delilah comes in many forms.

## **ANGER.**

The Bible says to be angry and sin not: let not the sun go down upon your wrath.[16] I now realize that I have been living in sin because I have been angry with my Lord most of my adult life and I have had to repent. Yes, I have been upset, doubtful and mad at God. Why? Being a believer is challenging. Being a believer is not just about going to church. It means to trust the Lord with your entire life—both the good and the bad, until death do us part. You should trust God when others question why you believe and follow, when things go wrong in your life, when others think you committed sin or caused the calamity, and you know God is moving. Even when something so traumatic has happened that could not have occurred except God gave the approval, or when you believe you are the servant, friend and the one who the Lord sends and He throws you for a loop you should trust Him.

Anger could set in for a long time if you are not careful and discerning. I have been angry, and it has affected my prayer life and my relationships. I could not understand why the Lord allowed me to get beaten up as a teenager. I cannot figure out why four people in my immediate family, including my mom, were taken from this world in a two-year period. I know God is sovereign, and I have heard that so many times, but words from people do not cause the pain and anger to go away. What is helping me is my faith that the Lord gave me to believe in spite of all the turmoil and tragedy, He has always been on my side.

I know there are many out there just like me. Whether it is the death of a close loved one, or divorce, or a traumatic experience or the feeling that you have been dealt a bad hand in this thing called life, I am here to tell you that the Lord loves you. I know it is hard to comprehend. A lot of the time you have questions as to why did such and such happen. Some things could shake your faith, but in spite of it all, the Savior came to redeem me back to Him, and He loves you just the same. The love of Christ is not conditioned upon the feebleness of our minds, but assured through all our messes.

---

[16] Ephesians 4:26

There are three passages of scripture that have kept me in this walk: **Psalms 27, Romans 8:28-39 and Philippians 4:6-8**. One encourages me, the other explains that I am a conqueror who nothing will separate from the Lord, and the last tells me how to think to obtain peace. You see, the Lord loves us so much that He places a battle plan with a roadmap in front of us. It is up to us to believe He is who He says He is.

Yes I have had a tough life, and yes I still have a lot of work to do on myself, but anger is no longer in control.

# A letter to the Pastor

Grace, mercy, and peace be unto you from God the Father and our Lord Jesus Christ. Most people go to church and expect to be guided to the Lord by the men and women that are called to be their pastors or ministers. It is as if there is an unspoken thought that the leader of the church should be the wisest, kindness, most emphatic, most loving, most giving one who practices the principles in the Bible even if no else does. The average church member or visitor who presses through the doors understands that the pastor is not perfect, but they do not want the leader to be like them. We all want shepherds.

I have been blessed to be around many men and women who are great shepherds. Thank you. Your sacrifice to the people in the church is honored. You pray and fast and sometimes place your family requests second to our perceived needs. We often watch you sacrifice your mental health, money, professional desires and body to get the Word of God to us. You are examples of Christ. Thanks much for your love.

I have also witnessed those who lack that gift. Please forgive me if I am out of line, but we would like you to be less selfish and protect the sheep. We need your help to grow closer to God. Of course we will not agree with everything you say but do not comprise the gospel to make us happy or to cause us to give a bigger offering. We expect you to step on our toes and keep us from falling off the cliff of sin. But, how can we sin less if you do not show us the way?

Guide us, teach us, model before us a posture of prayer. We watch you and see what to do and also what not to do. If you encourage us to pray more, we will. If you show love in the trials of life, we will follow that example and love others during our trials in life. If you are a male pastor, how strong is your men's ministry? If you are a woman leader, how chaste and loving are the females in your fellowship? Like sheep, we are what we are being fed and shown. There are a million churches in America, and we choose to join this one. Has the fellowship become more like God or the world?

If you are a married bishop or pastor, how does your family look? Has the mission of the Bride been compromised to fit into the world? Are we following the world's stance of being happy and doing what you like? How many leaders in the church are in broken homes? Are you, Bishop, Pastor, Elder, leading the local church in how a family is supposed to look?

I remember attending a church in Pennsylvania. Within a year, I became a leader in this small church, and my wife and I served in ministry. My marriage was going through some rough issues, and I asked the pastor to speak with us before the relationship got worse. I was shocked when the pastor told me that he did not have time to talk to us. Our church was small and, regardless of the size, I thought as a ministry leader my shepherd would counsel me. No such luck. When I objected, I was sent a letter and kicked out of the church. I was crushed. I have always heard about actions like this, but I never thought it happened. I am still amazed about some of the conduct. That was my church hurt story, but I can also tell you about some great and loving men and women of God also.

Bishop George Shorts, I tip my hat to you. You are a loving spiritual father to many of us. It was a joy serving in ministry under your leadership. The two and half hour drive to church each Sunday was worth it because I knew I was going to the house of the Lord and I knew I was being mentored and taught how to be a man of God. Being close to you as your adjutant, I got to see you up close and personal. You were not always perfect, but even in your transparency I saw uprightness and love. I remember many of the conversations we had as we drove together to a church where you were preaching.

*A letter to the Pastor*

I watched you skillfully pull me, my brother and all the men in our church closer to you and God. If someone had a barbecue, you were there. If a few men were going out to eat, most of the time you were there. You counseled us, skillfully put us in our place and then said *let's hang out*. I learned from you how to deal with adversity as a father and husband, and yet still display a godly standard. Thank you for being my mentor.

I also tip my hat to Pastor Ken. All I can say is in the short time I have known you, I experienced what the Word describes as the pastor being a *shepherd*. I can say that you love and care for us, and the character and integrity you display are that of a good man. Before you became my pastor, I knew I could trust you with my life.

Question, Pastors, how many people in your church have you mentored and caused to become leaders? Have you shared your gift to those in the ministry? Are you following the example of Jesus Christ in how he trained the disciples to be leaders and to spread the gospel? Can you share what you know about the Lord, life, marriage, and finances? Can you please train us? Christ taught his disciples how they should live. He challenged them, confronted the sin in their lives and kept them close to him. My brother, my sister, my pastor, what life lesson have you learned or deliverance have you acquired that can set one of us free that is bound? Are you afraid to be transparent with your life?

Pastor, we need you because you have the anointing for the work. The Word and testimony that the Lord has placed in you are there because you are one of our leaders. We need you because often the Spirit speaks the words of life to you first. What is the Spirit saying to families? What is the Lord speaking to you? Do you still have an ear to hear? We love you and will follow you, but we need you to proclaim His righteousness. Do you have a fresh, life-changing word for us? Can you admonish the congregation without fear of God's judgment for the same acts? We truly need your leadership because people in the church are dying, some are starving, we are thirsty, and a lot of us are tired. We need your leadership because we love you and because you are called.

# A letter to the Man

Brother ole brother, where are you? Have we totally trusted the proclamation of the gospel to our women and children? Where are we? Why are our churches filled with more females than men? Do we as a collective unit suffer from an identity crisis? Why have most of us forgotten, or don't we understand, that God has ordained us to lead? Please, brother, we have to get it together. We are dropping the ball, and there is no excuse for neglecting to proclaim the gospel and setting up the standard. The Word instructs us quite plainly who we are. The Bible states: "Watch ye, stand fast in the faith, quit you [be brave] like men, be strong."[17]

Has money or status become your god? Are you content with watching from the sideline, or is it fear or pride? That's right fear.

## **FEAR.**

So many good men would rather sit in the house by themselves instead of getting close to another man. Now I am not the most outgoing guy, and at times I can be somewhat of a loner, but I have grown to understand that there is strength in others. Not everyone is out to spread your business or harm you. The same problems and concerns you have, either one of us is going through it now, has been through it, or will go through it in the future. No one is perfect. You

---

[17] 1 Corinthians 16:13

may have an answer to many of the questions I have. I was once in a men's meeting where one of my friends stood up and bluntly said, "Look, if I am going to come to these meetings, dudes have to be real and speak their minds. If not, I can sit home with my wife and baby girls." That was the spark of something great. Men began to open up and share their worlds. To be transparent and express what you feel does not make you weak or a punk; we all have battles that are overbearing and make us vulnerable. And sometimes, we are afraid—scared of letting our women and children down, afraid that the money won't last, leery of dropping the ball again, or afraid that if people knew what you've done or said or where you came from, they wouldn't accept you. Just because the next guy appears to be polished and accomplished does not mean he is not also battling the same foe you are fighting. How would you know that unless you joined the brotherhood?

## **LIKE-MINDEDNESS.**

When I was in the streets, I knew who had my back: my people from East New York would live and die for you. We ate together and did dirt together. A few months ago I saw a few of them; I received hugs, and everyone was quick to tell me that they loved me. What am I saying? A lot of men in the church have forgotten the strong bond they once shared with other people. You knew if you messed with one, the other was coming for you. If you were missing in action, someone was going to find you and tell you to get your act together. Gangs in this country have grown so much because people feel that they belonged, and that others have their back no matter what.

The believers in the Bible ate, were put in prison, shared their clothes, resources and died together. If they knew that a brother had a need, everyone worked together. Even our Lord, when He sent out the disciplines, sent them out two by two. It is not meant for us to live and succeed in this life alone. That's why the Word says "one chase a thousand and two put ten thousand to flight."[18] The Word also states, "Iron sharpens iron."[19]

## **IDENTITY CRISIS.**

I have witnessed so many men afraid to voice their opinion. God has ordained us to lead. A lot of the issues faced by our families and the church are due to our silence or passing the buck.

---

[18] " Deuteronomy 32:30

[19] " Proverbs 27:17

# A letter to the Woman

Be strong in the Lord and the power of His might! There is a lot I could say to you, but the most important is thank you. For as long as I can remember, there have been more women in our church than men. You have supported the church financially, given your time, raised your children in the way and labored spiritually. In most ministries, men are the shepherds, yet our women have been faithful to the call and through Christ pushed the gospel through the world. Although I do not fit into this category, a lot of our men have dropped the ball, and I apologize for all of us.

In my home growing up, my dad was clearly the head of the house. It was evident in how we did everything as a family. I witnessed strength in my mom in submission to Christ and my dad. In my home, we had had weekly Bible study, and it was mandatory. When my cousins stayed overnight, they also attended the lessons and completed tests like us. Mom always prayed throughout the house and took us to church. My father would join us occasionally (Easter, Christmas, Mothers Day). When we had family meetings, mom prayed. Again I say I witnessed her strength in submission and in the manner in which she conducted herself.

My mom was a very strong black woman. She had to be to deal with my pops. If we needed discipline and Dad was not home, she would pinch us (her way of disciplining us). Sometimes all she had to do was look at us. Because of her love, we rarely acted up in her presence. This woman had a great godly love for our dad and us, which caused a house full of men to revere, love and submit to her. She did not waver in her commitment to Christ, and although my father did not accept Christ until right before his death, she led our home spiritually. Now I am not boasting; her model was not too unique back then. I witnessed countless women like her: my aunts Lori, Viola, and Annie. All too often the women, whether they worked or not, carried the spiritual mantle for a lot of homes. In doing so, they possessed a kind of grace. However, there is a difference now. The difference now is strength has a different name. For a whole lot of women, strength means, "Mister, you can't tell me anything because God is using me as well", "My money is equal or greater than yours", or "I have been doing this without you." Please do not misinterpret what I am saying because I still see a lot of biblically strong sisters now, but there is a new taste in the Kool-Aid.

# A letter to the Parent

As Christian parents, it is important to read the Bible to us and pray nightly. The only way we will know the Word, especially at a young age, is if you teach us. It is also important if we go to church every Sunday. How can we learn about God if you do not show us? We should also see you pray for family and friends.

My dad always taught me, no matter what's going on in life, to always look towards God. I have not been the best at connecting with God or praying to Him; but when somebody else I spoke to had problems, I would tell them to talk to God. I explained how the Lord always helps you through situations, but deep down inside, I was the person who needed God more.

I asked God to show me the way to be successful. I pray for my parents no matter what because I want them to be happy. The thing that hurts me the most is that sometimes my parents do not understand how I feel. I want my parents to be the best they can, but just care more about my feelings. If they were to step in my shoes, life would be different. Overall, more freedom would give us more explanations of the real world.

As parents, I believe that it is important for us to understand that our children live in a technology-based the world in which sin and pleasures of the flesh have more access to our offspring. A lot of the pressures and temptations our children face are in their pockets. Anything they want to experience is on the world wide web and social media. No longer does someone have to travel to encounter certain things. We have the greatest weapon: the Word of God. The Bible clearly instructs us to train up a child in the way he should go.[20] If we do not indoctrinate our children at an early age, tell them who they are, the heritage they have, where they are going and who they belong to, society and spiritual forces will attempt to place a label on them.

It is vital that you remind them as **necessary** that they are "a chosen generation and a royal priesthood."[21] They are "joint heirs with Christ."[22] They "can do all things because Christ strengthens them."[23] And "greater is he (the Holy Spirit) that is in them, than he that is in the world."[24]

---

[20] Proverbs 22:6

[21] " 1 Peter 2:9

[22] Romans 8:17

[23] Philippians 4:13

[24] I John 4:4

# Conclusion

It is our prayer that you received this book in love. Thank you for listening.

## THE PLAN OF SALVATION

| | |
|---|---|
| ACKNOWLEDGE | Romans 3:23 |
| REPENT | Luke 13:3 |
| CONFESS | Romans 10:9,10 |
| FORSAKE | Isaiah 55:7 |
| BELIEVE | John 3:16 |
| RECEIVE | John 1:12 |

**"Behold, I stand at the door, and knock: if any man hear my voice, and open the door, I will come into him, and will sup with him, and he with me" (Revelation 3:20).**

Dear Lord, be merciful to me, a sinner. I acknowledge my transgressions, and I repent of my sins. Forgive me, for I am willing to forsake my sins and live for you. I believe that you died for me, and I invite you into my heart by faith to be my Lord and master. Thank you for saving me.

I have followed the scriptural steps above, and today I received Jesus into my heart.

_____      _____

Name                                                                              Date